Discovering
RATS AND MICE

Jill Bailey

Illustrations by Wendy Meadway

Wayland

Discovering Nature

Discovering Ants
Discovering Bees and Wasps
Discovering Beetles
Discovering Birds of Prey
Discovering Butterflies and Moths
Discovering Crickets and Grasshoppers
Discovering Flies
Discovering Flowering Plants

Discovering Frogs and Toads
Discovering Hedgehogs
Discovering Rabbits and Hares
Discovering Rats and Mice
Discovering Snakes and Lizards
Discovering Spiders
Discovering Squirrels
Discovering Worms

Further titles are in preparation

All photographs from Oxford Scientific Films

First published in 1986 by
Wayland (Publishers) Limited
61 Western Road, Hove
East Sussex BN3 1JD, England

© Copyright 1986 Wayland (Publishers) Limited

British Library Cataloguing in Publication Data

Bailey, Jill
Discovering rats and mice—(Discovering nature)
1. Mice—Juvenile literature 2. Rats—Juvenile literature
I. Title II. Meadway, Wendy III. Series
599.32'33 QL737.R6

ISBN 0–85078–816–1

Typeset by DP Press Limited, Sevenoaks, Kent
Printed and bound in Italy by Sagdos S.p.A., Milan

Cover *A harvest mouse climbs among the brambles which are good to eat.*

Frontispiece *A harvest mouse climbs among the caterpillars on a ragwort plant.*

Contents

1
Introducing Rats and Mice

Bank voles are common in most parts of the countryside.

Origins and Relatives

Rats and mice are small, intelligent animals found almost all over the world. Some live in and around human homes. Others live in deserts, forests and mountains, far away from towns and cities.

Rats are bigger than mice, and have longer, more pointed snouts. Rats and mice belong to a large group of animals called **mammals**. They are covered in soft fur, and their bodies are always warm to touch, even in cold weather. Baby rats and mice are fed on milk produced by their mothers.

Rats and mice are related to squirrels, and also to guinea-pigs, beavers and porcupines. All these animals have small bright eyes, long whiskers and big front teeth. They are called **rodents**. Rodents gnaw their food, scraping at it with their long

The North American deer mouse lives almost anywhere. It can be found in grasslands, forests, deserts and mountains.

front teeth. Rats and mice do not have such stiff bushy tails as the squirrels, and they do not have such big heads and chunky bodies as the guinea-pigs.

The ancestors of rats and mice lived about 50 million years ago. They were squirrel-like animals. Their remains have been found in parts of North America. Since that time, rats and mice have spread across the world, and **adapted** to live in many different places. Today there are more than a thousand different kinds of rats and mice. In fact, there are more rats and mice than people in the world.

A mother harvest mouse and her babies in their nest. The female harvest mouse makes her nest from grass.

What Rats and Mice Look Like

Rats and mice are small, furry animals with bright eyes and rather pointed snouts with long whiskers. Most rats and mice have long scaly tails. They have short legs, and usually run along the ground on all fours.

All rats and mice have a pair of long front teeth in each jaw. These teeth are called **incisors**. They act like chisels for biting off grasses and scraping at nuts and seeds.

The long, stiff whiskers on the snout are very sensitive to touch. This is particularly useful for some kinds of rats and mice, which feed at night. Mice and rats also have a very good sense of smell. They use it to find food, and also to recognize friends and enemies. Many rats and mice have quite big ears. Their hearing is so good that they can make out sounds which we cannot hear.

The bodies of rats and mice are covered in fur though some have spines. There are two kinds of hair in the fur. The short soft hairs keep the animal warm. The long, rough guard hairs waterproof the fur, and protect

All rats and mice have a pair of long, sharp front teeth.

the skin from wear and tear. Most rats and mice are a brownish colour, and blend well with their surroundings. This makes it difficult for their enemies to see them.

Although rats and mice often live in dirty places, they are very clean animals. They spend a lot of time washing and **grooming** themselves.

The white-footed mouse of North America has bright eyes, a pointed snout, long whiskers, short legs and a long scaly tail.

2 Where Rats and Mice Live

The harvest mouse is an acrobat. It can climb among wheat stalks, gripping them with its feet and using its tail like an extra limb.

Fields, Meadows and Grassland

Grassy places are popular homes for rats and mice, since most of them feed on plants. Many rats and mice live around farms, where they are often pests, fouling corn in stores or stealing and eating the wheat in the fields.

In some parts of the world there are vast areas of natural grassland such as the prairies of North America and the steppes of central Europe. Here voles and lemmings are very common. They feed almost entirely on grass, and have short legs, and very short tails, since they do not need to be acrobatic.

These grasslands can be very cold in winter, and sometimes the grass gets buried by snow. Voles, lemmings and many other rats and mice live in underground burrows. Many of them also eat the underground parts of plants, like roots and bulbs, so they can feed without going out in the cold.

Lemmings can survive as far north as the Arctic Circle and beyond.

The dormouse hibernates during the winter, living off its stored fat.

The lemmings make tunnels in the snow. Here they are sheltered from the cold air above, and can still reach the grass below.

Hamsters and some other mice **hibernate** during the winter. During the summer they get very fat. They also store seeds and larger items like bulbs in their burrows. In the winter they curl up in their underground nests and go into a deep sleep, living off their fat. On warmer days they wake up and feed on their stored food. A single hamster has been found to collect as much as 90 kg (200 lb) of plant food in its burrow.

In the Desert and Under the Ground

Rats and mice are found even in very hot, dry places. They usually spend the day in their cool burrows, and come out to feed at night. There are not many places to hide in a desert, so it is safer (and much cooler) to wait until it is dark.

Nocturnal rats and mice have big eyes for seeing in dim light. They have big ears, and can hear four times better than humans can, well enough to hear the wing beats of an approaching hunting owl.

There is very little water in a desert. At night dew forms on leaves and

Jerboas can cover 3 metres in a single leap.

seeds, and the rats and mice get their water from eating these.

Desert rats and mice have to travel long distances to find enough food. Jerboas and kangaroo mice have long back legs and big hind feet. They hop like kangaroos, holding their long tails out behind them to help them balance. When resting, they use their tails as props.

Many rats and mice live in burrows in the ground. Some use their teeth to

A kangaroo rat in the Arizona desert.

dig away the soil. Others use their claws for digging. A few rats spend almost their whole lives underground. The molerats live in large, complicated burrows with many tunnels and rooms, and feed on underground roots and stems. One kind of molerat is completely blind. Since it lives underground, in the dark, it does not need to see.

The African dormouse is quite at home in the trees.

Forests and Woodlands, Rivers and Lakes

Forests and woodlands are home to many different kinds of rats and mice. Wood mice and wood rats live in burrows in the forest floor or in cracks in tree trunks and under tree roots.

Dormice and climbing rats and mice live up in the trees. Their little feet can curl round twigs, and their strong claws give them a good grip on bark. Some coil their tails around twigs and branches for extra safety. The scales on their tails usually lie flat against their skin, but if the tail starts to slip backwards, the scales pop up. This helps the tail grip the surface the animal is climbing.

Many rats and mice are good swimmers, and some choose to live beside lakes and rivers. Water voles make their holes in river banks, often with underwater escape routes.

The water vole stretches its chunky body into a streamlined shape for swimming under water.

The muskrat has a tail like the rudder of a boat which it uses to steer itself through the water.

The muskrat piles up water plants and mud to make a dome-shaped home in the water. Using its underwater entrances, it can swim and hunt for food under the ice in winter.

Rats and mice which swim a lot usually have small ears and **streamlined** bodies. The marsh rats and muskrats have webbed feet for swimming. Webbed feet are also useful for walking on wet mud.

Many water rats are good at catching fish. They also feed on other small water animals, such as shellfish and frogs, as well as on plants.

Living with Humans

For thousands of years rats and mice have lived with humans. Wherever humans live, there is food for rats and mice. There are crumbs, and food in dustbins and rubbish dumps. Rats and mice are pests. They steal our crops, raid our larders and chew up our papers and clothing. Even rats and mice that usually live out of doors will come into our houses in winter in search of warmth and food.

The house mouse probably started living with humans about 10,000 years ago, when people first began to grow **cereal crops**. Since then, it has spread almost all over the world, carried in bags of grain and packing-cases, on ships and trains.

The black rat has also lived with humans for thousands of years. It likes to live in the roofs of houses, and is often called the roof rat. People

Rats and mice often live in the holds of ships. They are good climbers, and can easily run ashore along mooring ropes. This is a black rat.

notice it because they hear its footsteps above them.

In the Far East, Australia and New Zealand, the Polynesian rat is the commonest house pest. Like the black rat, it is a good climber, and can raid birds' nests high up in trees.

The worst pest in Europe and North America is the brown rat. The brown rat is not as good at climbing as the black rat. It prefers to live in cellars and sewers. The sewer systems of modern towns and cities provide lots of homes for brown rats.

A brown rat searches for food in a rubbish dump.

3
Food and Feeding

A wood mouse searches for food.

How Rats and Mice Feed

The long front teeth or incisors of rats and mice help them to eat very tough foods. They can break open dry seeds and hard nuts, and even gnaw through electric wires. The incisors are very sharp, and because of the way they rub against each other, they sharpen themselves.

Because rats and mice eat rather tough foods, their incisor teeth get worn down quickly. To make up for this, the teeth keep on growing all through their lives.

At the back of the jaws are the cheek teeth, or **molars**. These are big flat teeth covered in bumps or ridges of enamel. They are used for grinding the food into very small pieces.

Between the incisors and the molars is a wide gap. The animal can draw its lips into this gap while it gnaws at its food. This stops sharp

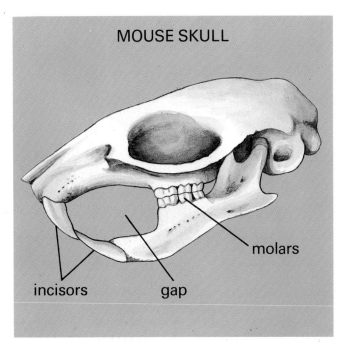

MOUSE SKULL

molars

incisors

gap

pieces of broken-off food going into the back of the mouth and being swallowed by accident.

Rats and mice have very flexible front feet, which they use to handle food. They can pick up seeds and berries, and use their fingers to peel open buds and fruits. While they feed, they turn the food round in their paws to get at the juiciest parts.

This dormouse is eating a chestnut. Notice how it holds the nut between its front paws.

Finding Food

Most rats and mice eat different kinds of plant food – seeds, nuts, fruits, leaves, and underground roots and bulbs. Many eat insects, too. Insects contain more **nutrients** than plants. Hamsters, gerbils, dormice and water rats eat frogs, baby birds and other small animals if they get the chance.

In many places, rats and mice eat different food at different times of the year. In spring and summer, there may be plenty of insects, leaves and tender young buds. In autumn, there will be nuts and seeds, while in winter they have to live off stored seeds, or dig for underground stems and roots.

Rats and mice have many enemies, so it is often safer to carry food to a sheltered place to eat it. Because they walk on all fours, they have to carry food in their mouths. Hamsters, African pouched rats and American

Hamsters can carry a store of food in their cheek pouches.

pocket mice have loose folds of skin in their cheeks which form pouches. When **foraging**, they push food into these pouches. Later, they empty them by squeezing the food out with their front feet. Hamsters can turn their cheek pouches inside out to clean them.

Most rats and mice do not have very good eyesight. They rely on smell to find their food. Many rats and mice feed at night when it is not so easy for their enemies to see them. Nocturnal rats and mice have big eyes, which can see in dim light. They also use their long whiskers as feelers to investigate their surroundings.

A spiny mouse of Kenya eating an insect.

4
Family Life

A pack rat's nest in the Mojave Desert in California. The pack rat is also called the wood rat.

Making a Nest

Some rats and mice are skilled builders. The European harvest mouse weaves a ball-shaped nest from grass. The round shape keeps the nest waterproof – the rain just runs off.

The wood rats, or pack rats, of North America and the stick rats of Australia build large untidy nests of sticks, twigs, and even cacti. The Australian stick rats put stones on their roofs to stop them blowing away.

Inside the house there are passages and chambers, food stores and special holes for droppings. Pack rats can store so many droppings in their nests that the droppings were once collected for fertilizer. Up to twenty sackfuls could be found in a single pack rat's nest.

The pack rats are great collectors. They love bright shiny objects like nails, silver ornaments, cans, glass, and even mousetraps!

Pet rats and mice usually seem to enjoy company, but this is not always true in the wild. Many rats and mice, including hamsters, live alone for most of the time. Some rats and mice live alone during the summer, but gather together to share a burrow or nest in winter. They huddle together to keep warm. Others like to have company all the time. Grasshopper mice live in pairs, while house mice and gerbils live in large groups.

Female hamsters build complicated burrows with lots of different tunnels and rooms.

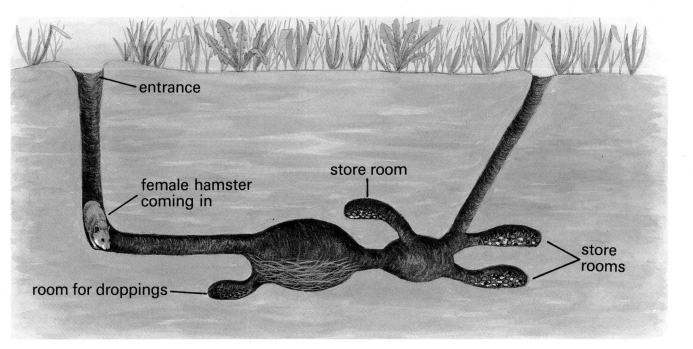

entrance

female hamster coming in

store room

store rooms

room for droppings

Talking to Each Other

Some rats and mice make their own separate nests, but live close together in the same place. Each mouse guards the area around its nest. This area is called its **territory**.

Sometimes they will fight for living space. The biggest, strongest animal wins. During these fights the mice do not usually hurt each other too badly. There are special signals, like looking away, turning the head, or crouching low, which tells a mouse that its opponent wants to surrender. Each mouse soon learns its place and avoids fighting with mice that are stronger.

Rats and mice make many squeaks which we cannot hear. They are too high-pitched for our ears. Gerbils, kangaroo rats and deer mice also drum on the ground with their feet. The wood rat thumps its tail against a tree so loudly that you can hear it 15 m (49 ft) away.

Rats and mice have other ways of 'talking' to each other. They use smell. Rats and mice recognize each other by their smell. Smell tells them whether

The house mouse lives in ready-made holes and cracks in houses.

another animal is the same kind of rat or mouse, whether it is male or female, whether it is frightened, and even whether it is ready to **mate**.

To tell other animals where its territory is, a rat or mouse may smear

These black rats certainly look as if they are having a conversation.

a smelly liquid around the edge of the territory. Or it may smear droppings or urine instead.

Courtship and Mating

Female rats and mice can mate when they are only a few weeks old. Male and female rats and mice are attracted to each other by their smells. They then go through various stages of courtship. Often the male chases the female. Then they get closer, and sniff and touch each other. When the female is ready, she lets the male climb on her back and mate with her.

Rats and mice often do not live for much more than a year. They make up for this by **breeding** very fast. The fastest breeder of all is the North American meadow mouse, which produces seventeen **litters** a year,

These courting male and female harvest mice are sniffing each other and touching whiskers

with around seven young in each litter. A single meadow mouse can produce over 100 young a year. But so many are caught by **predators** that the numbers of meadow mice do not change much.

Some rats and mice can breed all through the year. Others breed mainly in one season, usually when there is most food around. Some mice produce a litter every month.

Sometimes rats and mice breed too

A pair of house mice mating on a kitchen shelf.

quickly and run out of food. When this happens, large numbers of them may move away from the area in search of new feeding grounds. Lemmings do this frequently. Hundreds of lemmings may travel over long distances, climbing mountains and swimming rivers in their desperate hunt for food.

Bringing Up a Family

After mating, the female usually chases the male away. She brings up her family by herself. The male goes off to look for another female.

First the female rat or mouse makes a nest, usually of soft grass, feathers, or even chewed up paper. She chases off other mice that come near. About eighteen days after she has mated, the female harvest mouse gives birth to her babies, usually between three and eight of them.

The new born harvest mice are tiny, only about the size of your fingernail. They are blind, deaf and helpless. They have no fur at all, just wrinkled pink skin.

The baby mice feed on their mother's milk, which they suck from little **nipples** on her belly. After five days they start to grow fur, and by seven days their eyes are open and they can hear. Soon they are taking chewed up food from their mother's mouth.

By now the babies are growing fast. They are making short trips outside the nest with their mother and learning to find their own food. After

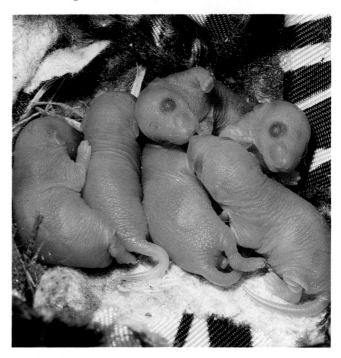

Above *Newborn mice are naked. Their eyes and ears are closed.*

about sixteen days the mother leaves them to go and build another nest for her next litter.

Until they are old enough to take solid food, baby mice feed on their mother's milk.

5
Staying Alive

Rats and mice have many enemies including birds like this owl.

Enemies of Rats and Mice

Rats and mice have many enemies. Animals which hunt other animals are called predators. On the ground, the main predators of rats and mice are weasels, stoats and foxes, but many other animals will kill very small rats and mice.

Rats and mice have their eyes at the sides of their heads. They can spot enemies coming from the side as well as from the front.

Running into a burrow is usually a good way of escaping. The burrows of rats and mice are often too small for predators to enter. Only snakes can get in. Some rats and mice can shed their tails if grabbed by a predator. Losing your tail is better than losing your life.

There is also danger from above. Many birds, like hawks and owls, eat rats and mice. Most rats and mice are

camouflaged – their coats match their surroundings. Grass mice even have stripy backs, so they match the grasses around them. The spiny rat has stiff spines in its fur, which makes it unpleasant to swallow. Where there is not much cover, many rats and mice come out to feed at night.

Gerbils have such good hearing that they can hear the wing beats of approaching owls. Some rats and mice warn each other of danger by stamping their feet on the ground. Others scream or whistle.

Above *Gerbils match the colour of their surroundings, so their enemies cannot see them easily.*

A mother rat or mouse will move her babies one by one to a safe place.

6
Rats, Mice and Humans

Rats and mice raid our food stores. This brown rat has found a sack of grain to eat.

Rats and Mice as Pests

Many of the crops grown on farms provide food for rats and mice. We grow grass for pasture, and wheat, barley, corn and rice for their seeds, and sugar cane for its sweet stems. These are just the things rats and mice eat. Every year, rats and mice eat over 40 million tonnes of food.

Farmers also store large amounts of grain and other food. Rats and mice live in the grain stores. Not only do they eat the grain, but they also contaminate it with their droppings. In a single day, 100 rats can produce 5,000 droppings.

Rats and mice are responsible for other kinds of damage, too. Rats burrowing into river banks and sewers have caused floods. They burrow under roads, making them collapse. When they gnaw through electric cables, they cause power

cuts and sometimes fires.

Over twenty different diseases are carried by rats. They include bubonic plague, typhus and food poisoning. In the last thousand years, these diseases have killed more people than all the wars and revolutions. Some, especially typhus and food poisoning, still present serious problems today.

Rats and mice steal our crops growing in the fields.

The plague, or Black Death, as it used to be called, killed over 25 million Europeans in medieval times. It is carried by rat fleas. When the rats die of plague, the fleas bite humans instead, passing on the disease.

Controlling and Using Rats and Mice

It is very difficult to control the numbers of rats and mice because they multiply so fast. The simplest control is to keep food and water out of their reach, tightly covered, and to keep pipes sealed so that rats and mice cannot live there. Cracks in buildings and furniture should be filled up so they will not provide homes for rats and mice.

Cats are often used to keep numbers down, but they can only cope with small numbers of rats and mice. Traps also work for small numbers, but the best way to kill large numbers of rats and mice is to poison them. They are very intelligent and soon learn to avoid poisoned food if it makes them feel ill. But if the poison takes a long time to act, they do not learn quickly enough.

Rats and mice are very important in medical research.

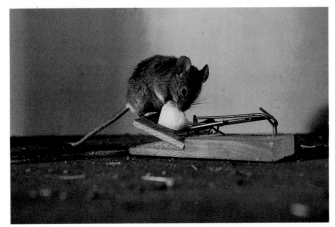

Traps can be used to catch small numbers of mice.

In some parts of the world people eat rats and mice. The ancient Romans used to eat dormice, and kept them in special pens to fatten them up.

The fur of the muskrat is used in North America and Europe to make clothes. It is called musquash.

Rats and mice are used to test drugs

A cat watching a house mouse in a bottle. Cats are good mouse-catchers.

to make sure they are safe for humans to use. Without these tests, we would not have made such progress in medicine. Drugs tested on rats and mice save millions of lives every year.

7
Learning More About Rats and Mice

It is often easy to spot the burrows of rats and mice. These holes were made by Kangaroo rats which live in the desert areas of North America.

In the Wild

It is not easy to see rats and mice in the wild. Many of them only come out at night. Others are so well camouflaged that they are difficult to spot. They are very timid and will disappear down their burrows if they hear you coming.

To see wild rats and mice, you have to look for clues. Often it is easy to spot their holes. But are these holes occupied? Look for droppings near the entrance. The droppings are quite small, only 2 or 3 mm across. Look for runways in the grass. Rats and mice use the same paths when they come out to feed, and this flattens the grass.

If you find a used hole, try waiting to see if the animal comes out. You have to be very quiet and still. Try not to sit up-wind of the animal. Rats and mice have a very good sense of smell and can smell you long before you can see them.

Put some food out such as cheese or bread. Try not to handle the food, otherwise it will have your smell, and the rat or mouse may not go near it.

Where the ground is soft, look for footprints and other tracks, like these mouse tracks in the sand.

When they feed, rats and mice leave bits of chewed seed husks and broken nuts around. The way in which the nuts have been broken open can tell you what kind of animal has been feeding on them. In houses, mice and rats leave a trail of damage: chewed papers, nibbled food packets, and often smelly droppings.

Rats and Mice as Pets

Rats, mice, hamsters and gerbils all make good pets. Pet rats, mice and hamsters come in many different colours, but gerbils are always the same sandy colour.

Mice and gerbils like to have company, but hamsters are used to living alone, and will fight with other hamsters. If you want to keep more than one animal, keep males and females in separate cages unless you want to breed them.

Rats, mice and hamsters usually sleep during the day. In the evening they wake up and feed and play. Gerbils are active most of the time.

Your pet will need lots of seeds and

Gerbils make good pets because they are active most of the time.

fresh green plant material to eat, as well as a fresh supply of drinking water. Hamsters and gerbils usually put some of their food in a special place to eat later.

Because rats and mice have very sharp teeth, you need a cage of strong material like metal or plastic. You can buy suitable cages in pet shops. In the wild, their teeth are worn down all the time by the tough food they eat. Pet rats and mice need to have something hard to gnaw on, otherwise their teeth will grow too long.

All rats and mice like to have soft material like paper, sawdust and wood shavings for burrowing in and making nests. This also helps to

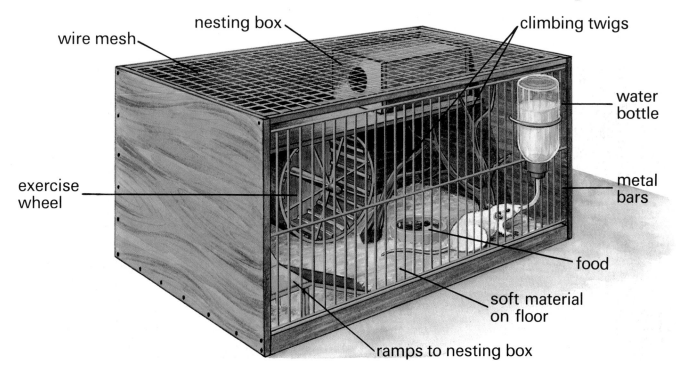

nesting box

wire mesh

climbing twigs

water bottle

exercise wheel

metal bars

food

soft material on floor

ramps to nesting box

absorb their waste. Watch a pet hamster fill its cheek pouches with paper and take it to its nest.

Rats and mice need exercise, so an exercise wheel is a good idea, and some twigs or branches to climb on. They are very intelligent animals, and should have things to play with. Rats will always take the shortest route to food, so try making a maze for them to solve before they get the food.

Most rats and mice only live for two or three years, so try not to get too fond of your pet.

Below *Rats and mice like to explore new objects.*

Right *You will not be popular if your pet escapes to explore the house!*

Glossary

Adapted Changed so as to become better suited to a particular way of life.

Breeding Producing and rearing young.

Camouflaged Having a colour or pattern which matches the background and makes the animal difficult to see.

Cereal crops Any grasses grown for their edible seeds, such as wheat, maize and rice.

Foraging Searching for food.

Grooming Licking, scratching and smoothing the fur to clean it.

Hibernate To sleep through the winter.

Incisors Long, front, cutting teeth shaped like chisels.

Litter A group of baby animals all born at the same time, from the same mother.

Mammals Warm-blooded animals with hair or fur, the females of which produce milk to feed their young.

Mate The way in which male and female animals join together to produce young.

Molars Broad, flat, back teeth used to grind and chew food.

Nipples Small teats on the bellies of female mammals, through which the young suck milk.

Nocturnal Active at night rather than by day.

Nutrients Substances in food which are needed for the growth and health of the animal.

Predators Animals which kill and eat other animals.

Rodents Members of a group of mammals which have large, chisel-shaped front teeth for gnawing.

Streamlined Shaped for travelling fast through water or air.

Territory A piece of land occupied by a particular animal that defends it and tries to stop other animals from coming into it.

Finding Out More

If you would like to find out more about rats and mice you could read the following books:

R. Whitlock, *Rats and Mice* (Wayland Publishers, 1974).

J. Coldrey, *Nature's Way – Harvest Mouse* (André Deutsch, 1981).

S. Harris, *The Harvest Mouse* (Blandford Press, 1980).

R. Hill, *The Usborne First Book of Pets and Petcare* (Usborne Publishing, 1982).

E. Hurrell, *The Common Dormouse* (Blandford Press, 1980).

J. Lawrence, *Pet Guides – Hamsters* (Hamlyn, 1984).

K. Lawrence, *Pet Guides – Gerbils* (Hamlyn, 1984).

Oxford Scientific Films, *House Mouse* (André Deutsch, 1977).

Index

Picture Acknowledgements

All photographs from Oxford Scientific Films by the following photographers:

T. Allen 31; A. Bannister 33 (right); G.I. Bernard *cover, frontispiece*, 9 (bottom), 12, 15, 28, 33 (left), 35; J.A.L. Cooke 14; D. Curl 10; S. Dalton (NHPA) 13 (right); J. Dermid 24; M.P.L. Fogden 38; B.P. Kent (Animals Animals) 9 (top), 11; T. Levin (Animals Animals) 32; D.W. MacDonald 36 (right); B. Milne (Animals Animals) 17 (right); S. Morris 23; Press-tige Pictures 8, 17 (left), 19, 20, 22, 34; A. Ramage 40; R. Redfern 18, 27; D. Thompson 26, 29, 30, 36 (left), 37, 39, 42, 43; P. & W. Ward 16; B.E. Watts 21; G.J. Wren 13 (left).